Contents

James Naismith believed that the fun and action of sports could improve the lives of young people.

Tough Love and a Tough Life

Winter in Canada can be very hard. Icy wind sweeps down from the north. Rivers freeze solid. Crossing them can be scary and dangerous.

James Naismith turned eleven in 1872. He was old enough to know where the river near his home became safe, solid ice. But he took a shortcut he had never tried before. His team of horses pulled his wagon onto the frozen river. Their feet pounded the ice. Then one heavy hoof slammed through the sheet of ice. James jumped off the wagon and landed in the water. Grabbing the horses by their reins, he pulled hard. The horses were fighting him. Slowly he forced them through the broken ice to the other side of the river. The horses and the boy were so wet that icicles formed on them.

James grew up near Almonte, Ontario, in Canada.

James looked around. He saw his uncle Peter Young watching him from behind some trees. But his uncle had not helped him. Uncle Peter wanted James to learn to solve problems by himself and not to take foolish chances. It was a tough lesson.

James was born on November 6, 1861, near Almonte, Ontario, which is in Canada. When he was almost nine, his father, John Naismith, came down with deadly typhoid fever. So they

This is the city of Almonte, Ontario, in Canada, as it looked in the early twentieth century.

would not catch the disease, James, his sister, Annie, and brother, Robbie, were taken to their grandmother's home. A few days later, their father died. Two weeks later, their mother, Margaret, died of the same disease. A short time later, their grandmother Annie Young died of old age.

That left Uncle Peter to take care of the children in Bennie's Corners, near Almonte.

The village had a schoolhouse, a blacksmith shop, a store, and lots of other kids to play with. There was a swimming hole with a muddy hill for sliding right into the water. There were bunches of boys who loved wrestling and running. The children had lots of fun with very little money. When James needed ice skates, he made them. He took two strips of old, rusty metal and sharpened them. He pounded the metal strips into two wooden boards and tied the boards to his shoes. Then he raced out onto the frozen swimming hole like a champion skater.

After his parents died, James moved to this house, which belonged to his uncle Peter.

The best game in town was called duck on a rock. One player, the guard, would put a rock about the size of his fist on top of a great big rock near the blacksmith shop. The other boys threw stones at the "duck" to knock it off the big rock. If they missed, they had to pick up their stone before the guard could tag them. It sounds easy, but it is not. The pitch could be soft, but it had to be perfectly aimed. When a player missed the duck, there was a lot of running, shouting, and laughing. James would remember duck on a rock years later when it would be very important to him.

James and his friends used this big rock to play their favorite game, duck on a rock.

James (right) and his best friend, R. Tait MacKenzie, loved to spend time outdoors.

Chapter 2

The Dropout

James was great at sports. He also worked hard on the family farm. He did not work hard at school, though, and his grades were never very good. He wanted to grow up fast and be a man with a job. When he was fifteen, he left school and worked as a lumberjack. He cut down trees for almost five years. Then he decided to change his life.

James had a plan. He wanted to go back to high school and finish fast. His next step would be college. His sister and his uncle Peter wanted him to work on the farm. They argued. Finally they made a deal. James could go to college if he promised to study and become a minister after he graduated. He also promised to come home to work on the farm every summer. In 1883, James entered McGill University in Montreal, Canada.

When James was home for a visit, his brother, Robbie, had a terrible pain in his side. They all thought it was just a stomachache. It was actually a very bad infection. Robbie died a few hours later. A doctor could have helped him. Knowing Robbie might have been saved stayed in James's mind every day of his life.

In 1887, James graduated from McGill University after studying Hebrew and philosophy. Hebrew is an ancient language that many ministers study. Philosophy teaches people to think about life. James had a lot to think about.

James (front) won two sports awards at McGill University.
Here he is with the gymnastics team.

Chapter 3

The Minister Plays Hardball

For James, the next step was studying to become a minister at McGill's Presbyterian College. There was much to learn, and he studied day and night. His friends tried to get him to play sports. They told him it would sharpen his mind and toughen up his body. He said no and kept on studying.

One day his strong friends dragged him out to the football field. James had so much fun that from then on he found time to study hard and play hard, too. He was smaller than the other players, but he was powerful and smart. He learned rugby, which is a very rough game. He loved lacrosse, which can be even rougher.

One Saturday James got two black eyes in a wild game of lacrosse. The next day was Sunday,

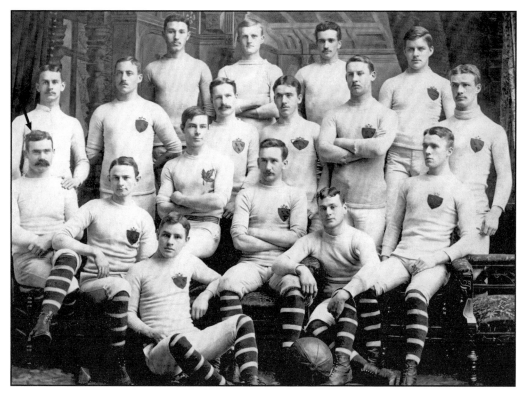

James (far left, seated) joined the rugby team at McGill University.

and he had to give a sermon in the church. James, the student minister, looked out from behind those two black eyes. He may have looked kind of funny, but he finished the sermon he had written.

In 1890, James became a Presbyterian minister. But he did not want to give sermons in a church. He thought he could help teens live better lives if he talked to them while teaching them sports. His sister and his uncle Peter were deeply disappointed. James was sorry, but he believed in his idea.

James taught at the YMCA training school from 1891 to 1895.

His first sports job was at the International YMCA Training School, which is now Springfield College. So he moved from Canada to Springfield, Massachusetts, in the United States.

James signed up for the football team. The coach, Amos "Alonzo" Stagg, had been a famous football player at Yale University. He watched James smashing through the other teams' players. Stagg picked James for a very rough position on the team. He said, "Jim, I play you at center because you can do the meanest things in the

The football team at the YMCA training school poses in the uniforms used in games. Players in those days did not wear pads or helmets. James (front row, second from left) and Alonzo Stagg (center, with ball) became good friends.

most gentlemanly manner." Stagg admired the way James was rough and tough but never nasty.

As a student teacher, James was very good at the job of teaching baseball, field hockey,

James (left) plays football with Stagg. James, who invented the football helmet, is wearing an early model.

football, and rugby, which are great games during spring, summer, and fall. Winter was a problem. The men had to come indoors and exercise, which was not much fun. They were so bored that some of them wanted to quit the YMCA training school.

James was told to invent an exciting indoor game. It had to be ready in two weeks. That was the deadline.

Chapter 4

Inventing Fun

James struggled with the problem for twelve days. The game had to be fast and fun. It could not be risky, like football or rugby, with teams of men banging into the gym walls. James did not want rough tackling. He did not want people running with the ball. He did like the idea of throwing a ball at something. But throwing a ball hard indoors could be dangerous.

That good old game from his childhood, duck on a rock, flashed into his head. He remembered how using a soft pitch was the best way to aim for the "duck." James's eyes lit up. He shouted out loud, "I've got it!"

There was no time to invent new gear. Two peach baskets were used as goals. James explained the strange rules. Two teams of men dragged themselves onto the gym floor, grumbling. They took a soccer ball and started playing. The grumbling soon stopped. Cheers and shouts filled the gym. The date was December 21, 1891. Basketball was born.

Peach baskets were used as basketball goals before nets.

James Naismith had invented the great game all by himself. He was crazy about sports. Basketball fascinated him. Even so, he was not interested in coaching. He just wanted people to play for fun.

Soon teams formed in gyms all around town. In schools across the United States, students began to play basketball. Women began playing, too.

20

A young woman named Maude Sherman was on one of the first women's teams. James and Maude soon became friends, and then fell in love. They married on June 20, 1894. James and Maude would have five children together.

In a few years, basketball started being played more like it is played today. The peach baskets changed to rope baskets. Backboards were added. Dribbling became popular because players were not allowed to hold

1. The ball may be thrown in any direction.
2. It can be batted with hands, but not with the fist.
3. No running with the ball.
4. Hold the ball only with the hands.
5. No holding, pushing, hitting, or tripping the other team's players.
6. Follow the rules or a foul will be declared.
7. Make three fouls and the other team is given a goal.
8. A goal is made when the ball goes into the basket.
9. When the ball goes out of bounds, the first person to touch it, or the umpire, will throw it onto the court.
10. The umpire is the judge of the players. He can call fouls.
11. The referee is the judge of the ball. He decides on goals.
12. Game time is two fifteen-minute halves.
13. The team with the most goals in that time is the winner.

Maude Sherman was on one of the first women's basketball teams.

the ball very long without throwing it. When the ball bounced off the floor as a player raced down the court, it sounded like a fast drumbeat. James thought dribbling was a great idea.

In 1895, James and Maude moved to Denver, Colorado. There James became director of physical education at the largest YMCA in the country.

He was always working on his plan for the future. He remembered his brother dying horribly without help from a doctor. He had seen athletes have terrible accidents. He wanted to be a doctor and help people.

The First Basketball

George L. Pierce invented the basketball used today.
Here is his sketch for the patent.

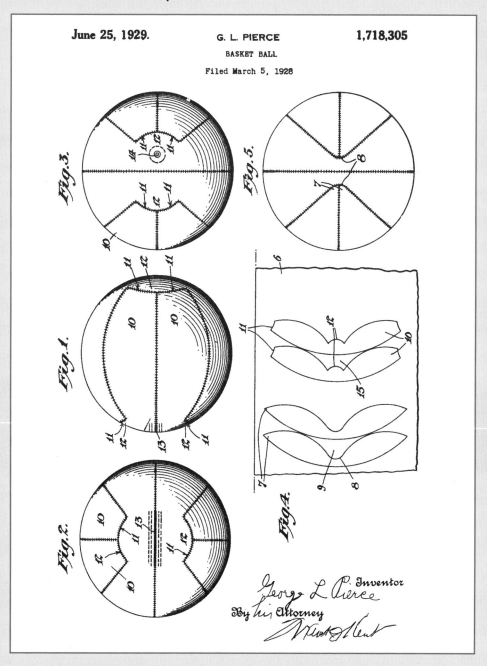

There was no stopping James when he had a plan. He became a student at Gross Medical College in Denver. He would work all day at the YMCA and then study to be a doctor after work and on weekends. James graduated as a medical doctor in 1898.

In 1892 baskets did not have a backboard.

That year he got the job of assistant physical director at the University of Kansas. By 1909 James was working there as a minister, a professor, and a medical doctor.

James called this women's team, the Edmonton Commercial Grads, the finest example of a basketball team. They were world champions for seventeen years in a row.

Chapter 5

The World Stood and Cheered

James became the chaplain of the First Kansas Infantry during World War I.

In 1916, James became a minister in the United States Army. The next year, the YMCA sent him around the world to help American soldiers in World War I. On May 5, 1925, the sixty-three-year-old Canadian became an American citizen.

In 1936, James was invited to the Olympic Games in Berlin, Germany. It was the first time basketball was an official game in the Olympics.

Basketball teams played from countries all over the world. The players all spoke different languages. But they all wanted to shake hands with the inventor of basketball.

James Naismith could have made lots of money by selling sports equipment. He could have used his fame to pose for ads selling products. He refused the offers. He just wanted to do his job as a teacher, minister, and sports doctor.

Basketball was first played as an Olympic sport at the 1936 Olympic Games.

By the time basketball was one hundred years old, millions of basketball fans were cheering their favorite teams and players. Hoops were hanging in many backyards.

The Philippines beat Mexico 32–30 in a second-round match at the 1936 Olympics. Mexico would go on to win the bronze medal, while the Philippines would make it to fifth place.

And street games were being played in cities all over the world.

James Naismith died of a heart attack on November 28, 1939, at age seventy-eight. He had been given a tough problem to solve in just two weeks. He invented a special kind of fun that has become popular all around the world. He believed his sport could make the lives of young people better. And he was right.

1861   Born on November 6, near Almonte, Ontario, Canada.

1870   Parents die; moves to Bennie's Corners, Ontario.

1887   Graduates from McGill University in Montreal, Quebec, Canada.

1890   Becomes a Presbyterian minister.

1891   Invents basketball at the International YMCA Training School in Springfield, Massachusetts; first game is played December 21.

1894   Marries Maude Sherman on June 20.

1895   Becomes director of physical education at YMCA in Denver, Colorado.

1898   Graduates as a medical doctor from Gross Medical College in Denver; becomes assistant physical director at the University of Kansas.

1909   Is professor, minister, and doctor at the University of Kansas.

1917   Helps American soldiers in World War I as a military chaplain.

1925   Becomes United States citizen.

1936   Is honored at Olympic Games in Berlin, Germany.

1939   Dies on November 28 in Lawrence, Kansas.

blacksmith—Someone who heats and hammers iron into different shapes like nails and horseshoes.

chaplain—A minister in the military.

college—A school people go to after high school to study a certain subject, like math or writing.

dribbling—Bouncing a basketball off the floor.

minister—Someone whose job it is to talk to others about faith.

rugby—A team sport in which each player can kick, pass, or run with the ball, and tackle the other team's players.

sermon—A talk about faith, usually given by a minister in a church.

typhoid fever—A deadly disease that can be caught from eating or drinking unclean food or water.

university—A school made up of more than one college.

YMCA—**Y**oung **M**en's **C**hristian **A**ssociation. The YMCA is a group that helps people to live healthy and good lives.

Books

Eule, Brian. *Basketball for Fun!* Minneapolis, Minn.: Compass Point Books, 2003.

Hareas, John. *Basketball.* New York: DK Publishing, 2005.

Thomas, Keltie. *How Basketball Works.* Toronto: Maple Tree Press, 2005.

Thomas, Ron and Joe Herran. *Getting into Basketball.* Philadelphia: Chelsea House Publishers, 2005.

Internet Addresses

Naismith Museum and Hall of Fame
www.naismithmuseum.com

History of Basketball
www.kansasheritage.org/people/naismith.html

A

Almonte, Ontario, 6, 7

B

backboards, 21
basketball
   first ball design, 23
   first game, 20
   original rules, 21
Bennie's Corners,
   Ontario, 7
Berlin, 26

D

Denver, Colorado, 22, 24
doctor, 12, 22, 24, 27
dribbling, 21, 22
duck on a rock, 8–9, 19

F

football, 14, 16, 18, 19

G

Gross Medical College,
   24

H

Hebrew language, 12

I

ice skates, 8

International YMCA
   Training School, 16,
   18
invent a game, 18–19

L

lacrosse, 16
lumberjack, 11

M

McGill University, 12,
   14
minister, 12, 14, 15, 24,
   26, 27

N

Naismith, Annie (sister),
   7
Naismith, James
   American citizen, 26
   died, 28
   five children, 21
   married, 21
Naismith, John (father),
   6
Naismith, Margaret
   (mother), 7
Naismith, Robbie
   (brother), 7, 12

O

Olympic Games, 26

P

peach baskets, 19, 21
philosophy, 12
Pierce, George L., 23
Presbyterian College, 14
professor, 24

R

rugby, 14, 18, 19

S

Sherman, Maude (wife),
   21–22
Springfield,
   Massachusetts, 16
Stagg, Alonzo, 16–17

U

University of Kansas, 24
U.S. Army, 26

W

women basketball
   players, 20–22

Y

YMCA, 16, 18, 22, 24, 26
Young, Annie
   (grandmother), 7
Young, Peter (uncle),
   6–7, 11, 16